MW00814276

MORE FREAKY STORIES ABOUT THE PARANORMAL

YES **OUIJA** NO
REG. U.S. PAT. OFF.
THE MYSTIFYING ORACLE
REG. U.S. PAT. OFF.

ABCDEFG...LM
NOPQRSTU...XYZ
1234567890

BY JILL KEPPELER

Gareth Stevens
PUBLISHING

Please visit our website, www.garethstevens.com. For a free color catalog of all our high-quality books, call toll free 1-800-542-2595 or fax 1-877-542-2596.

Library of Congress Cataloging-in-Publication Data

Names: Keppeler, Jill, 1974- author.
Title: More freaky stories about the paranormal / Jill Keppeler.
Other titles: Freaky stories about the paranormal | Freaky true science.
Description: New York : Gareth Stevens Publishing, [2020] | Series: Freaky true science | Includes bibliographical references and index.
Identifiers: LCCN 2019003296| ISBN 9781538240700 (pbk.) | ISBN 9781538240724 (library bound) | ISBN 9781538240717 (6 pack)
Subjects: LCSH: Parapsychology–Juvenile literature. | Curiosities and wonders–Juvenile literature.
Classification: LCC BF1031 .K3775 2020 | DDC 130–dc23
LC record available at https://lccn.loc.gov/2019003296

First Edition

Published in 2020 by
Gareth Stevens Publishing
111 East 14th Street, Suite 349
New York, NY 10003

Copyright © 2020 Gareth Stevens Publishing

Designer: Sarah Liddell
Editor: Therese Shea

Photo credits: Cover, pp. 1, 7 (Ouija board) andrea crisante/Shutterstock.com; cover, p. 1 (foot) Anna Rassadnikova; cover, p. 1 (tail used throughout) IADA/Shutterstock.com; cover, background throughout book Shukaylova Zinaida/Shutterstock.com; hand used throughout Helena Ohman/Shutterstock.com; paper texture throughout Alex Gontar/ Shutterstock.com; p. 5 Balate Dorin/Shutterstock.com; pp. 9, 10, 19 Bettmann/Contributor/ Bettmann/Getty Images; p. 11 dnaveh/Shutterstock.com; p. 13 Lee Boxleitner/ Shutterstock.com; p. 15 Nebojsa Markovic/SHutterstock.com; p. 17 Joseph Sohm/ Shutterstock.com; p. 18 Stock Montage/Contributor/Archive Photos/Getty Images; p. 21 Drone Explorer/Shutterstock.com; p. 23 Tohma/Wikimedia Commons; p. 25 Athanasios Gioumpasis/Contributor/Getty Images News/Getty Images; p. 27 (main) Fœ/Wikimedia Commons; p. 27 (inset) Oregonian2012/Wikimedia Commons; p. 29 Alexlky/ Shutterstock.com.

Printed in the United States of America

CPSIA compliance information: Batch #CS19GS: For further information contact Gareth Stevens, New York, New York at 1-800-542-2595.

CONTENTS

Words in the glossary appear in **bold** type
the first time they are used in the text.

PRESERVED IN PICTURES

Have you ever seen a weird light or a floating ball in a photograph? Sometimes, people have paranormal explanations for such things. Something might be considered "paranormal" if it's strange and can't be easily explained by science. Paranormal ideas include aliens, ghosts, and legendary creatures.

Some people believe glowing orbs in photographs—round specks of light—show the presence of spirits or **psychic** energy. However, many photographers and scientists say there's an ordinary explanation: backscatter, which is how light reflects off tiny particles in the air. These particles are nearly invisible to the human eye, but when light from a camera flash hits them, the camera captures them. In this book, you'll learn about other paranormal **phenomena** and some possible explanations for them. You can decide if you believe in the paranormal!

FREAKY FACTS!

Orbs can be caused by specks of dust, pollen, bugs, rain, or snow. If they're close to the camera lens, they're unfocused.

4

YOU CAN TEST PHOTOGRAPHING ORBS YOURSELF. TAKE A CAMERA, GO INTO A DARK PLACE, AND KICK UP SOME DUST. START SNAPPING AWAY!

PHOTO PHENOMENA

People use other photographic phenomena as evidence of the paranormal, too. They'll show photos that have ghostly images of people in them, odd faces in otherwise normal scenes, and streaks of unexplained light. However, each of these images can be explained by other means, too: film in a camera that's been double exposed (combining two images into one), reflections in mirrors and windows, the human tendency to see faces, and camera error.

OUIJA!

If you walk into a toy store today, you may be able to find a Ouija (WEE-jeh) board on the shelf with the board games and puzzles. That seems like a very ordinary spot for an item with a long, strange history. Ouija boards first appeared for sale in 1891, created by a group of businessmen who'd read about "talking boards" used by **mediums** to communicate with the dead.

To use a Ouija board, each person taking part puts a hand or hands on the planchette, which is the small piece that comes with the bigger board. The planchette slides across the Ouija board, pointing at letters, numbers, or words. Sometimes, it seems to spell things out or send a message!

FREAKY FACTS!

Some people say the name "Ouija" comes from the French and German words for "yes"—*oui* and *ja.* However, another story says the makers of the board asked it for a name. Supposedly, it said "Ouija."

HOW DOES IT WORK?

Over the years, Ouija boards have been considered mere games, real tools for contacting spirits, and dangerous occult devices. Today, however, scientists say they're truly powered by the people who are using them, even if those people don't realize it. People make small muscle movements without knowing it, and these "ideomotor" movements make the planchette move. So, the truth is, Ouija boards may be delivering messages—but they're just messages from ourselves!

THE OUIJA BOARD

YES

NO

YES OUIJA NO

PLANCHETTE

ALPHABET

NUMBERS

OUIJA BOARDS WERE SOMETIMES USED BY MEDIUMS DURING A SÉANCE, WHICH IS A MEETING WITH THE PURPOSE OF COMMUNICATING WITH THE DEAD.

BIGFOOT AND FRIENDS

There are many different names for large, hairy monsters that supposedly live in remote areas of the world—Bigfoot, Sasquatch, Yeti, Abominable Snowman, and Skunk Ape are just a few of them. Some people point to photos, footprints, and eyewitness accounts to prove that these creatures exist. There have been movies and TV shows made and books written about the hunt to find them. Some think Bigfoot and similar creatures could be a link to mankind's **primate** ancestors.

However, most scientists say scientific proof is needed—and there isn't any yet. Some Bigfoot sightings have turned out to be hoaxes. Many turned out to be bears or other wildlife. **Skeptics** say that if creatures that are so large exist, someone would have real evidence of them by now.

FREAKY FACTS!

A cryptid is an animal that has been claimed, but never proven, to exist. A cryptozoologist is a person who hunts for these animals.

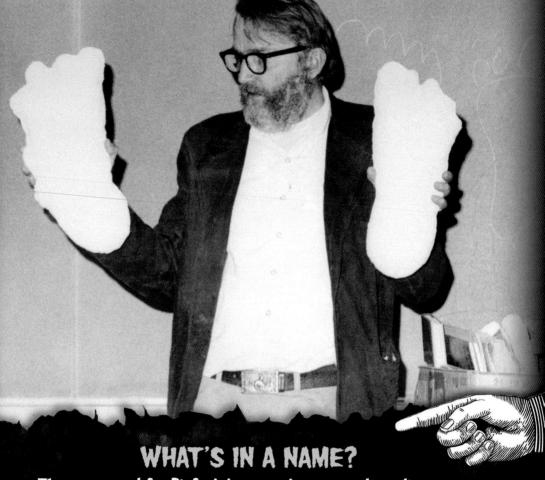

ANTHROPOLOGIST GROVER KRANTZ IS SHOWN HERE IN 1974, WITH CASTS OF FOOTPRINTS THAT HE SAID WERE MADE BY SASQUATCH IN WASHINGTON STATE. KRANTZ SAID THE CREATURE WOULD BE ABOUT 8 FEET (2.4 M) TALL AND WEIGH 600 TO 800 POUNDS (272 TO 363 KG).

WHAT'S IN A NAME?

The names used for Bigfoot-type creatures vary depending on where stories of sightings are from. The names Bigfoot and Sasquatch are used for creatures seen in the northwestern United States and western Canada, while the Yeti and Abominable Snowman hail from the Himalayas. Skunk Ape stories are from Florida and other parts of the southern United States. The Yowie is from Australia. Some believers say similar stories throughout the world are a sign that Bigfoot is real.

One of the most famous pieces of evidence for Bigfoot believers is the Patterson-Gimlin film. Bob Gimlin and Roger Patterson shot this short film in 1967 in the woods of northern California.

FREAKY FACTS!

The Patterson-Gimlin video has 59.5 seconds of footage of the creature. You can find it online if you want to see for yourself.

It seems to show a big, hairy, ape-like figure walking on its hind legs. The beast briefly pauses to look back at the camera before disappearing into the trees. Some people think it's a hoax, but Gimlin and Patterson swore that it wasn't.

Whether the stories are true or not, the hunt for Bigfoot and other cryptids has helped science in a few ways. Scientists have **analyzed** samples of hair from creatures suspected to be Bigfoot—and learned more about the DNA of the creatures that actually provided the sample.

THE SCIENCE OF NESSIE

Bigfoot isn't alone in inspiring scientific discovery. In 2018, scientists started collecting DNA from the lake called Loch Ness in Scotland. It's home to legends about a dinosaur-like monster, sometimes called "Nessie," said to live in its waters. Scientist Neil Gemmell said he doesn't believe in the creature, but he knows the tales get people excited about science. His studies may be able to tell us a lot about the creatures that do live in the lake.

THE MYSTERY HOUSE

The Winchester Mystery House in San Jose, California, has been called one of the most haunted places in the world. But what's really going on at this 160-room mansion? That's probably far more complicated—and maybe even more interesting than ghosts!

Sarah Winchester inherited the fortune of the Winchester firearm-manufacturing company. In 1886, she had workmen start building a mansion out of a farmhouse—and then constantly added to it until she died in 1922. One popular explanation for the weirdness of the house, according to a 1911 newspaper article, is that Sarah believed she had received "a message from the spirit world." It told her "all would be well as long as the sound of hammers did not cease in the house or on the grounds."

FREAKY FACTS!

Magician Harry Houdini visited the Mystery House in 1924. He planned to debunk its ghost stories, but still puzzled, he gave it its name!

THE WINCHESTER MYSTERY HOUSE HAS DOORS AND STAIRCASES THAT GO NOWHERE, HALLWAYS SAID TO BE HAUNTED, AND THE NUMBER 13 REPEATED IN ITS DESIGN.

THE REASONS WHY

We'll never know why Sarah truly had the house built in its unusual fashion, but she did believe in spiritualism, the belief that the living can talk to spirits through mediums, which was very popular at the time. She'd lost both her husband and her baby daughter in the years before she started the house and may have believed messages she supposedly received from mediums she'd used while trying to contact them.

ZOMBIE SCIENCE

Just about everyone's probably seen or read a story about zombies, people brought back from the dead without their own willpower or speech. In most stories, they stagger around, looking for brains to eat, attacking the living. But zombies are just stories—right?

The root of zombie stories may be in the Vodou religion of Haiti, but there are possible scientific explanations, too. Some parasites can influence how creatures act, taking away willpower. One, called *Toxoplasma gondii*, can only reproduce inside the body of a cat. So, when it's in other small creatures, such as rats, it makes them seek out cats. At that point, of course, they're generally eaten by the cats. The parasite can then complete its life cycle inside the cat.

FREAKY FACTS!

The US Centers for Disease Control and Prevention (CDC) started a website for "zombie preparedness." It began as a joke, but offers people tips to prepare for any emergency.

ZOMBIE WALKS HAVE BECOME POPULAR AROUND THE WORLD. PEOPLE GET DRESSED UP AS ZOMBIES AND WEAR ZOMBIE MAKEUP.

FREAKY FUGU

Another scientific phenomenon that provides background for zombie stories starts with tetrodotoxin, the poison from fugu, a kind of deadly puffer fish. This poison can kill people, but sometimes, it slows down or stops their breathing and muscle function for a time. They can't move or speak, and they may appear dead. Some people in Haiti may have used this poison and other ingredients to make people appear to be like zombies raised from the grave.

15

THE LOST COLONY

In human history, there are many stories about people disappearing. Most of these people—about 95 percent—return or are found at some point. Nearly 100 percent of the time, there's an explanation for the disappearance. However, in a very small percentage of cases, no sign of the person or any explanation can be found. Some people blame alien **abductions**, time travel, or other paranormal phenomena.

One famous missing-person mystery concerns the first try at creating an English colony in North America. Settlers established the colony in 1587 on Roanoke Island, off the shore of what's now North Carolina. Later that year, John White, governor of the colony, returned to England for supplies. When he returned in 1590, the colonists were gone.

FREAKY FACTS!

In 1586, English explorer Sir Richard Grenville left 15 men on Roanoke Island. When colonists arrived a year later, no one was there. White said, "We found the bones of one of those fifteen."

HAUNTED BANKS

Some people say the Outer Banks of North Carolina are haunted. The former site of the Roanoke colony is one legendarily spooky location. Others include Teach's Hole (where stories say Edward Teach—also known as Blackbeard the pirate—was executed), several **allegedly** haunted lighthouses, and the so-called Graveyard of the Atlantic, the waters along the North Carolina coast where many ships and sailors met their end.

THIS GRAVESTONE ON ROANOKE ISLAND HONORS THE COLONISTS WHO VANISHED FROM THE COLONY THERE. YOU CAN VISIT THE SETTLEMENT SITE TODAY AND SEE WHAT LIFE WOULD HAVE BEEN LIKE THERE.

Those looking for the lost colony found no bodies and no houses—only the word "Croatoan" and the letters "CRO" carved into trees. "Croatoan" is the name of both an island to the south of Roanoke and the Native American people who lived there. Some people think the colonists may have moved there or been attacked by the natives. Some think something even more mysterious might have taken place—that the settlers were killed by nature spirits, abducted by aliens, or even eaten by zombies!

The Roanoke colony was home to Virginia Dare, the first English child born in North America. Some stories say that her spirit lives on in the form of a white doe, or female deer, and can still be seen on the island today.

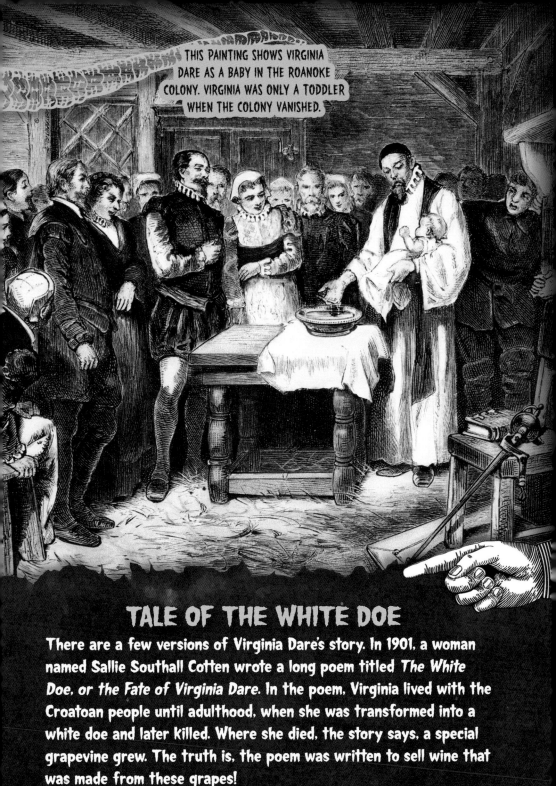

This painting shows Virginia Dare as a baby in the Roanoke colony. Virginia was only a toddler when the colony vanished.

TALE OF THE WHITE DOE

There are a few versions of Virginia Dare's story. In 1901, a woman named Sallie Southall Cotten wrote a long poem titled *The White Doe, or the Fate of Virginia Dare*. In the poem, Virginia lived with the Croatoan people until adulthood, when she was transformed into a white doe and later killed. Where she died, the story says, a special grapevine grew. The truth is, the poem was written to sell wine that was made from these grapes!

STANDING STONES

You may have heard of Stonehenge near Salisbury, England, but do you know why this circle of standing stones is there? Neither does anyone else! Archaeologists know that the site has been used as a burial ground, but beyond that, there are many other theories—some quite freaky!

Some people have proposed that Stonehenge is a sort of ancient computer, used to calculate when eclipses would take place. Some think it was a place of healing magic. Others say it was a landing site for UFOs! At least one researcher thinks it may have been constructed to produce a sound **illusion** in which sound waves cancel each other out to create a quiet place in the middle. It's also possible it may have been an observatory from which to watch the stars.

FREAKY FACTS!

The Stonehenge site faces the sunrise on the summer solstice. People still celebrate the solstices there today. More than 1 million people visit the site each year.

OLD STONES

Stonehenge's sandstone blocks are called sarsens. The biggest ones are about 30 feet (9 m) tall and weigh about 25 tons (23 mt). Prehistoric peoples built the monument in stages between 3000 and 1520 BC, although there are structures at the site that date back to 7000 or 8000 BC. Today, there are about 50 sarsen stones remaining and about 43 smaller stones, called bluestones. There were probably many more of both at one point.

PEOPLE HAVE MANY IDEAS ABOUT HOW THE HUGE STONES USED TO BUILD STONEHENGE WERE TRANSPORTED THERE. SOME WERE MOVED ABOUT 160 MILES (257 KM)!

THE DANCING PLAGUE

Do you like to dance? Even if you do, you probably can only dance so long before you get tired and have to take a break. In July 1518, a "dancing plague" struck the people of Strasbourg, which is a city that is part of France today. It started when a woman named Frau Troffea started to dance in the street. Sounds fun, right? However, she seemed unable to stop and kept dancing until she collapsed from exhaustion. Before she did, though, dozens of other residents had joined her, all unable to stop.

By August 1518, up to 400 people had joined in the dancing. Some died from heart attacks or strokes because they danced for so long! Doctors blamed the plague on evil spirits or "overheated blood."

FREAKY FACTS!

When town leaders couldn't figure out what was causing the plague or how to stop it, they decided the answer might be more dancing—and brought in a band! That didn't help.

THE PEOPLE OF THE STRASBOURG AREA ALSO BELIEVED IN SAINT VITUS, WHO COULD CURSE PEOPLE BY FORCING THEM TO DANCE.

THE SEARCH FOR ANSWERS

The dancing plague also happened, to a lesser extent, in other places. Today, some historians think the plague may have been caused by extreme stress. Strasbourg was going through some bad times, with widespread disease and shortages of food, and that may have started a mania, a sort of mental illness, that swept through the city. It's also possible the dancers ate food tainted, or affected, with ergot, a fungus that can cause medical problems.

CITY BENEATH THE SEA

Even today, stories tell of an island that sunk beneath the sea—the lost city of Atlantis. The legends may have started with the philosopher Plato more than 2,300 years ago. He wrote that the island, located in the Atlantic Ocean, had a rich, powerful civilization with great military might. However, its people became greedy and wicked, and the people's gods sent earthquakes that caused the island to sink beneath the waves. That was allegedly 9,000 years even before the time of Plato.

A few scientists have tried to link Atlantis with real locations, but most today say it's a myth. However, tales such as the one of Atlantis may have a basis in science. Plato lived in a time and place with earthquakes, volcanoes, and tsunamis.

FREAKY FACTS!

In 2017, a survey showed that more than half of Americans believed that "ancient advanced civilizations, such as Atlantis" existed.

GEOMYTHOLOGY

Scientists sometimes use the term "geomythology" to describe the science of how legends can rise from real geological events. About 3,600 years ago, a huge volcano erupted on the island of Santorini (or Thera), near Greece, causing earthquakes and tsunamis. This natural disaster caused great damage, including on the nearby island of Crete. This real event may have a link to the story of Atlantis.

A LITTLE MERMAID—SORT OF

Mermaids, half human and half fish, have been a part of legends for thousands of years. Mermaid images and stories are still popular today. As with many other paranormal phenomena, many people like to believe they're real—and as with other phenomena, there's a basis in fact for the legends. Some scientists believe that people saw manatees, a kind of marine mammal, and thought they were mermaids.

Entertainer P. T. Barnum cashed in on the public's fascination with mermaids back in the 1840s. He fooled many people with the mummified creature on display in his New York City exhibit and tripled attendance. However, the body was really the top half of a monkey with the tail of a fish sewn to it!

FREAKY FACTS!

There was more than one so-called Fiji mermaid, although Barnum's is believed to have been destroyed in a fire. You can still see some of them in museums today.

BARNUM CREATED A LONG STORY TO GO WITH HIS "FIJI MERMAID." HE HIRED A MAN TO POSE AS A PROFESSOR AND CLAIM THE MERMAID WAS CAUGHT NEAR THE FIJI ISLANDS IN THE SOUTH PACIFIC.

MODERN-DAY HOAX

In 2012 and 2013, the television station Animal Planet aired programs that claimed to show that mermaids were real, and the government was covering up the news. The shows looked quite real and convincing, and some people didn't realize that they were fake. So many people believed them that the US National Oceanic and Atmospheric Administration issued a statement saying that "no evidence of aquatic humanoids has ever been found."

CRIMES AGAINST CATTLE

Starting in the 1970s, stories of cattle being killed and mutilated, or badly cut up, have been reported in the United States. Parts of the bodies are often missing, with very clean-looking cuts, and the bodies are drained of blood. Some people think that aliens, monsters, or secret government operations are the cause.

However, scientists and investigators who have studied the cases say that normal predators or disease likely killed the cattle. Predators probably ate some parts. Then flies ate the softer bits and cleaned up the edges of any tears caused by predators. Maggots, which are immature flies, drank the blood.

People love mysteries like the ones in this book. Sometimes the scientific explanations aren't quite so fun. This is one reason why stories of the paranormal will continue to be popular!

FREAKY FACTS!

The US government investigated the cattle-mutilation phenomenon. They found no evidence of a paranormal cause.

SOME PEOPLE BLAME THE CHUPACABRA, A MYTHICAL ANIMAL OF THE AMERICAS, FOR CATTLE MUTILATIONS. CHUPACABRAS ARE SAID TO BE BLOODSUCKERS.

ARTIST'S IDEA OF A CHUPACABRA

MARSHALL'S EXPERIMENT

In 1979, Arkansas sheriff Herb Marshall got a number of calls about cattle mutilations in his area. Marshall decided to do an experiment. He took a dead cow, put it in a field, and filmed it for 48 hours. The cow started to decompose, or break down because of natural processes. The elements, insects, and other animals also did their work. After that, it looked just like the other "mutilations."

GLOSSARY

abduction: the act of taking a person away by force

allegedly: said to have happened but not proven

analyze: to find out what something is made of

debunk: to show that something is not true

illusion: something that looks or seems different from what it is

medium: someone said to be a channel of communication between the earthly world and a world of spirits

occult: related to supernatural powers or practices

phenomenon: a fact or an event that is observed

primate: any animal from the group that includes humans, apes, and monkeys

psychic: relating to supernatural abilities, energy, or knowledge

skeptic: a person who questions or doubts something

solstice: the time of year when the sun is farthest north (the summer solstice, about June 21) or farthest south (the winter solstice, about December 21) of the equator

stress: a state of concern, worry, or feeling nervous

FOR MORE INFORMATION

BOOKS

Greathouse, Lisa, and Stephanie Kuligowski. *Unsolved! Mysterious Places*. Huntington Beach, CA: Teacher Created Materials, 2013.

Martin, Michael. *The Unsolved Mystery of Atlantis*. North Mankato, MN: Capstone Press, 2014.

WEBSITES

Stonehenge Facts!
natgeokids.com/au/discover/history/general-history/stonehenge-facts
This website offers many photos and facts about the ancient monument.

Winchester Mystery House
winchestermysteryhouse.com
The website for the Winchester Mystery House has photos of the construction and stories about the house's history.

Zombie Preparedness
cdc.gov/cpr/zombie/index.htm
The Centers for Disease Control and Prevention uses this mostly joking site to educate about disaster preparedness.

INDEX